A Day in the Life of a...

Footballer

Harriet Hains

W

FRANKLIN WATTS

NEW YORK • LONDON • SYDNEY

Neil Adams is a footballer.
He plays for Norwich City Football Club.
The day before a match, Neil arrives at the
training centre at 9.30 a.m.

First the physiotherapist checks over Neil's leg muscles. "There's no sign of that knee injury, now," he says as he massages Neil's leg.

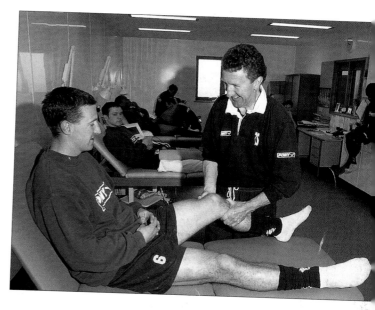

Next Neil works out in the gym. He uses an exercise bike to help him keep fit.

3

At 10.30 a.m. the 'squad' go outside to warm up. They start with some stretching. Then they sprint and jog around the pitch.

"Let's get moving, lads!" shouts John the coach.

4

"Keep those legs working really hard!" the coach tells the players.

Next the squad practise 'dribbling'. Each player guides a football between markers as quickly as he can.

After 15 minutes warming up, the coach organizes the players into two teams. Playing a practice game is a good way to train for a match.

Neil plays on the right wing.
He runs fast and 'shoots' to try to
score a goal.

Once the game is over, Neil goes to the canteen for his lunch. He always eats food that gives him lots of energy and helps to keep him healthy.

After lunch Neil has a shower and
gets changed. Then he leaves the
training centre and goes home to
relax until the next day.

9

It's the big day! Everyone at the football stadium prepares for the match. The groundsmen make sure the pitch is smooth.

In the stadium shop fans look at the team's strip.

From 2 p.m. the supporters begin to arrive. The team mascot says hello to the fans as they take their seats.

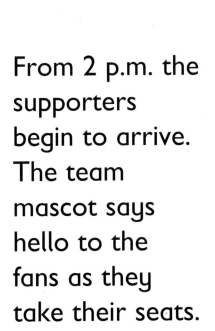

At 2.30 p.m. Neil and the rest of the team are changed and ready. They come onto the pitch to warm up. "Can I have your autograph, Neil?" asks one fan.

The players start stretching, running and jumping. "There's a large crowd today," says John. "Let's not disappoint the fans!"

"Come on the Canaries!" chants the crowd. "We want Norwich City!"

After their warm-up the team go back into the changing room until 3 p.m. Then the match starts. The crowd cheers as the teams run onto the pitch.

"Come on, Neil!"
shouts a fan as he
takes a corner.
Norwich City score.
"It's a goal!"
roars the crowd.

Neil passes the ball quickly and dodges in and out of the opposite team.

At half-time the score is 3-0 to Norwich. The crowd shouts with delight.

It's time for both the teams to rest. The fans relax and watch the entertainers.

Soon the second half begins.
Neil and his team play hard. They score
two more goals. Norwich City have won
the match 5-0!

At the end of the game, the team thanks the fans for their support. Neil leads the way as they walk around the pitch.
"What a score," Neil says.
"Today's match has been brilliant!"

How to exercise safely

Do you play a sport? Are you warming up properly? It is important to warm up all your muscles before any exercise. You must remember to cool down afterwards too. This is the way to do it properly:

1. Start by stretching your legs.

2. Then swing your arms around to get your blood flowing quickly to your fingers.

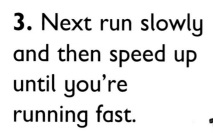

3. Next run slowly and then speed up until you're running fast.

4. When your muscles are warmed up you are ready to play!

5. After your game, gently walk about to cool down. Shake your arms around and shake each leg.

Take care!
If you don't warm up your muscles before exercise you can easily pull or strain them.

Facts about football

1. A football game is usually 90 minutes long. There is a half-time break of 15 minutes.

2. The players always use a new football for a league match.

3. All the team's gear is kept in a special room called a kit room. This is always locked until just before a game.

4. Footballers eat food that makes them strong and healthy. This means that they have a low fat diet with lots of carbohydrate such as pasta, bread and potatoes. They also drink plenty of water during a match.

5. The referee always signals the start and end of a game by blowing his whistle.

Facts about footballers

Neil is a professional footballer. This means that playing football is his full-time job. To become a professional footballer you need to play very well for your own school or Sunday youth team. You will hopefully be spotted by a professional football club's scout and invited for a trial at the club.

A successful trial means you will play for the football clubs' Academy of Soccer up to the age of 16. After this, you may be chosen for a 3-year football Academy Scholarship and play for the club's youth team. The club will watch your progress at football during this time and decide if you are good enough to become a professional.

Index

© 1999 Franklin Watts

Franklin Watts
96 Leonard Street
London
EC2A 4RH

Franklin Watts Australia
14 Mars Road
Lane Cove
NSW 2066

ISBN: 0 7496 3311 5

Dewey Decimal Classification
Number: 646.7

10 9 8 7 6 5 4 3 2 1

A CIP catalogue record for
this book is available from the
British Library.

Printed in Malaysia

Editor: Samantha Armstrong
Designer: Louise Snowdon
Photographer: Chris Fairclough
Illustrator: Nick Ward

With thanks to: Neil Adams,
John Faulkner, Val Lemmon
and everyone at Norwich City
Football Club.